WHO CREATED ME?

Written by: Benjamin Marshall

Illustrated by: Aadil Khan

Copyright 2020
by Passion Publications of Tell the Truth International

Who created me?

God of heaven

God created man in his own image, in the image of God he created him; male and female he created them. Genesis 1:27

WHY DID GOD CREATE ME?

To know Him and make Him known

For we are his workmanship, created in Christ Jesus for good works, which God prepared beforehand,
that we should walk in them.
Ephesians 2:10

WHAT DOES GOD THINK ABOUT ME?

He loves and values me.

Even the hairs on your head are counted. So, don't be afraid!
You are worth much more than many sparrows.
Luke 12:7

WHAT PURPOSE DID GOD CREATE ME FOR?

I must ask Him and He will show me.

I know the plans I have for you, to prosper you and not to harm you, to give you a hope and future.
Jeremiah 29:11

WHAT DOES GOD REQUIRE FROM ME?

To believe on Jesus, His Son and to obey His word.

Jesus answered, "'Love the Lord your God with all your heart,
with all your soul, and with all your mind."
Matthew 22:37

WE ARE ALL GOD'S CREATION BUT WE ARE NOT ALL GOD'S CHILDREN

Some, however, did receive him and believed in him; so, he gave them the right to become God's children.
John 1:12

JESUS, GOD'S SON CAME FROM HEAVEN TO EARTH

I didn't come from heaven to do what I want.
I came to do what the Father wants me to do. He sent me.
John 6:38

HE LIVED HIS LIFE IN SERVICE TO GOD

The Son of God came for this purpose:
to destroy the devil's works.
1 John 3:8

HE DIED ON A CROSS FOR ALL HUMAN SINS

But God demonstrates His own love toward us, in that while we were yet sinners, Christ died for us.
Romans 5:8

HE CAME BACK TO LIFE FROM THE DEAD

He was shown to be the Son of God when he was raised from the dead by the power of the Holy Spirit. He is Jesus Christ our Lord.
Romans 1:4

IF WE WANT TO BE GOD'S CHILD, WE MUST BELIEVE IN HIS SON, JESUS CHRIST

And they said, "Believe in the Lord Jesus, and you will be saved, you and your household." Acts 16:31

WE CAN NOW HAVE ETERNAL LIFE IF WE TRUST IN HIM.

"For God so loved the world, that he gave his only Son, that whoever believes in him should not perish but have eternal life."
John 3:16

WE CAN GO TO BE WITH HIM IN HEAVEN WHEN WE LEAVE THIS EARTH

When everything is ready, I will come and get you, so that you will always be with me where I am .John 14:3

Dear God,
I want to accept Jesus into my heart. I want him to be my personal Savior today. Jesus, I ask you to make me your child today. Thank you so much.

ABOUT THE AUTHOR

International teacher, speaker, and humanitarian, Benjamin Marshall is founder of Seeds of Truth Academy. His ministry and educational center extend worldwide. He has been blessed with four natural children and many God children.

*For other books and information contact him:
sotacademy@gmail.com*

www.ingramcontent.com/pod-product-compliance
Lightning Source LLC
Chambersburg PA
CBHW080120020526
44112CB00037B/2814